# The Covenant

# DAVID AJAERE

The Covenant

Copyright © 2015 David Ajaere

All rights reserved. No part of this publication may be reproduced, stored in a cloud or retrieval system, or transmitted, in any form or by any means, electronic, mechanical, photocopying, recording or otherwise, except as expressly permitted by law, without the prior written permission of the author.

ISBN: 978-0-9927882-1-6

Scripture extracts taken from *Holy Bible (KJV)* by Paul Avery, 2015.

Published by David Ajaere.
Printed in the United Kingdom.

• • •

Website:
www.risingofGodarmy.co.uk

Please give feedback on this book to:
davidajaere@risingofGodarmy.co.uk

# Dedication

• ✝ •

**I thank God for my life** and the privilege given to me by Almighty God to write this book. I dedicate this book to believers and to all God's Army preaching the true gospel of our Lord Jesus Christ to make a difference in our world today.

I have learned to become a man of strength with the army of Christ, through their examples, set out before me as I grew in Christ. They not only taught me how to work in faith and prayer, but they insisted that I live a life of holiness before God.

I have observed them, and my persistence and sheer determination in life has made me the man I am today.

I would like to express my sincere appreciation to Pastor Chris Oyakhilome, Pastor Uche Onubogu, my mother and father, Maria & Fred A. Okocha, Pastor Joel Osteen, Brother Lenga Odimba and my lovely wife, Mrs Sofia A. Okocha, along with my children.

• • •

# Table of Contents

Introduction ......................................................................... 9

Covenant ........................................................................... 13

False Covenant ................................................................. 29

Covenant Relationships .................................................... 43

Prayer ................................................................................ 51

Vision ................................................................................. 55

# Introduction

# Introduction

**God's word is our daily manual** that teaches and guides us throughout our life. When we read the word of God (in the Bible) it unveils His plan and purpose for our life in this world on earth.

I was praying so hard, believing in God, for a good change in my life. During this prayer, God revealed to me the false covenant that acts against my life. He specifically instructed and directed me through prayer and gave me guidance on how I can stop this false covenant from speaking against me.

Please note; whenever a covenant is broken, it becomes false. So I started to pray and research what *false covenant* means and what the Bible tells us about covenants. It was mind-blowing. What I discovered about the covenant was much larger than what I had thought – hallelujah. The word covenant is powerful; there's a spiritual force backed up by a covenant and the Bible tells us God is a covenant keeper.

## THE COVENANT

God wants us to enter into a covenant with him whenever we pray. By doing this you make it easier for your prayer to be answered. It means you really know what you are praying about or asking God to do for you. The Bible tells us he is a covenant-keeping God, so I encourage you, brethren, if you want God to answer your prayers quickly, enter into a covenant with God Almighty. And remember, when you do, keep your covenant with God – don't break it. You will see God in action. Your prayers requests will be answered. He is God of everything and everything belongs to Him.

> *And God said unto Abraham, Thou shalt keep my covenant therefore, thou, and thy seed after thee in their generations.* (GENESIS: 17-9)

...

# Covenant

# Covenant

• ✝ •

**A covenant is an agreement** or contract made between two parties. Backed up by the heavenly forces from the most high God, it is also defined as the spiritual agreement between Man and God. The Hebrew word for covenant is *berith*, derived from a root word which means 'to cut'.

So, a covenant refers to the practice described in the Old Testament of cutting or dividing an animal in two and then both parties passing each part between them to seal the agreement. Both parties vow that if they violate the terms of the agreement, it will be done unto them as was done to the animal.

> *When Abram was ninety-nine years old, the Lord appeared to him and said, "I am God Almighty; walk before me faithfully and be blameless.*
>
> *Then I will make my covenant between me and you and will greatly increase your numbers."*

*Abram fell facedown, and God said to him, "As for me, this is my covenant with you: You will be the father of many nations. No longer will you be called Abram; your name will be Abraham, for I have made you a father of many nations. I will make you very fruitful; I will make nations of you, and kings will come from you.*

*I will establish my covenant as an everlasting covenant between me and you and your descendants after you for the generations to come, to be your God and the God of your descendants after you.* (GENESIS 17:1-7)

Wow, brethren, how many of you would like to enter into and maintain a covenant with God by confessing Jesus Christ as your lord and personal saviour, and by believing that He died on the cross of Calvary for the remission of your sins? Have no doubt in your heart; God's covenant to Abraham is already in operation in your life... all you need to do is maintain the covenant's lineage in your life. The Bible says we are Abraham's seed that can never perish. We are set for the rising of God's Army in the land of the living.

In the spiritual realm, a covenant is well respected both within the kingdom of darkness and the kingdom of light. All spirits respect the covenant if you keep the covenant.

The devil dares not come your way because he knows what a covenant is about. He knows that he will surely fail if he tries, especially if you are covenanted with God Almighty.

For example, the Bible tells us about a man called Job. He was covenanted with God Almighty in all aspects of his life. When he was rich or when he was poor, he always bowed to God. He told himself he would never stop praising God, even when he was sick. Job maintained his peace with God. He refused the council of the wicked. His wife put pressure on him to commit sins or curse God, but he refused and he kept his covenant with God Almighty. So what happened? In the end, the Bible tells us that God rewarded Job with a hundred-fold increase in blessings because he was a faithful and righteous covenant keeper.

*And when Abram was ninety years old and nine, the Lord appeared to Abram, and said unto him, I am the Almighty God; walk before me, and be thou perfect. And I will make my covenant between me and thee, and will multiply thee exceedingly.* (GENESIS: 17-1-2)

Another good example from the Bible is Abraham's story. He worked with God Almighty and was covenanted with Him. The Bible tells us that God entered into a covenant with Abraham and He said to him, 'Leave your father's house and go to a foreign land.' He promised Abraham that he and his descendants would inherit the land and in that land God would bless him and make him prosperous. The Bible tells us that Abraham kept his own part of the covenant with God. He worked faithfully with God and the Bible records him as a father of faith.

Abraham became such a rich and influential man that he dined with the king of the land. He was well respected and had many servants working for him. You can see it pays off when you keep the covenant you enter into, either with man or with God. When you keep your covenant, blessings are waiting for you at the Altar of Obedience. When God gives instructions to someone, He waits for them to carry out those instructions. God will bless them once they have obeyed Him in the way He has instructed.

*God said to Abraham I will make of thee a great nation, and I will bless thee, and make thy name great; and thou shalt be a blessing: And I will bless them that bless thee, and curse him that curseth thee: and in thee shall all families of the earth be blessed.* (GENESIS: 12-2-3)

Brethren, I do not know what covenant you have entered into with people – for example, in your marriage, your workplace, with God, etc. – but please endeavour to keep your covenant and always be conscious of any covenant you have entered into.

Let me use this opportunity to share a short story of my life based on a covenant.

When I was a teenager, I entered into a covenant with a girlfriend whom I thought would be my future wife. I made her a promise that I would marry her, but later I travelled abroad and I was unable to keep the covenant I made to her. It was now broken and became a false covenant that spoke against my married life.

This story may educate you, especially if you are young. Be very careful not to enter into a covenant in any circumstance you find yourself in. I repeat… do not enter into a covenant that you cannot keep. You may feel that you are in control, but first ask God if you are really making the right decision. Is your partner ordained to be your wife or husband? Are you sure? Do you love him or her? These are the questions you should ask yourself before making that covenant.

God revealed to me that 70 per cent of people living in this world today are suffering as a result of broken covenants. It has eroded their God-given destiny without them even knowing the cause of their problem. They try to move forward in life but it always goes around and around in circles, circles, circles – a false covenant is speaking against them. I will explain.

I was in a relationship with a young lady. We were so

in love that I didn't want to think about what God might have said about the relationship I was having with this young lady. I vowed in my heart that I would marry her at all costs, even when God foretold me through a pastor that the lady was not to be my future wife. I did not believe him. I asked myself how God can say these kinds of things to me. I didn't believe it. It seemed impossible because the connection I had with her was strong. We really understood each other and I thought I was clever. I quickly entered into a covenant with her. I said to her, 'I will marry you at all costs.' She trusted me and took me at my word because I was the kind of man who always kept my word. When I said I would do something, I would do it, just as I had said. I think this was what motivated her to believe so faithfully in me. I was totally convinced she would be my wife; I had absolutely no doubt in my mind.

But a year into our relationship something happened and I had to travel out of the country. My plan was to return after six months and to marry her as I had promised. But it was impossible. My plan was in ruins. I needed to remain overseas. During those four good years abroad, I came to a realisation and I remembered what God had said to me through the pastor: that she was not to be my wife. But before then, I had already made a mistake by entering into my promise of marriage to her. Later, still while overseas, I sent a message to her through my mother. I told her that if she found another suitor who was interested in marrying her, she should go ahead and marry. I told her I didn't really know how long I would stay away because things were not working out as planned. I understood that she was heartbroken. I just broke the covenant I had with her, without knowing that that broken covenant would now become a false covenant speaking against me and working against my destined life path.

Afterwards, when I visited my home country, I had already met my present wife. I married her. We were deeply in love, though we had difficulty understanding each other. We are still in love and neither of us is willing to separate from each other. Even after seven years together as husband and wife, we would suffer because of our continued lack of understanding. I often felt fed up and frustrated, and I really wanted to understand what was happening to our marriage.

I fervently began to place our marriage problems into prayer study to hear the word of God. Then God opened the eyes of my spirit, enabling me to see that my problem stemmed from a false covenant speaking against me. Until I did something about it, I would not know peace in my marriage. Now that I knew my problem, God spoke to me and instructed me to look for my ex-fiancée to ask for her forgiveness. If I was forgiven, I might have peace and understanding in my marriage. I had to find her.

My investigations began through my sister and my friend. I found out that she was married and was still unhappy with me because of my broken covenant with her. I asked for her telephone number. I called her. I cried and pleaded for forgiveness and mercy. She finally forgave me. She blessed my children and my marriage. Since that day, my marriage has been restored.

Brethren, I don't know who you have entered into covenants with. It may be with God, in your marriage or with something else. If it is for a good cause, please, I encourage you to keep your own side of the covenant – it will surely produce multiple and happy blessings in all areas of your life. During any covenant in your life, it may look like you are passing through the wilderness, but do keep that covenant. Satan may come in different forms and try to make you break your covenant – but keep it. Burning Satan knows all too well the consequences of breaking a covenant. This is what The Lord has said.

> *The uncircumcised man child whose flesh of his foreskin is not circumcised, that soul shall be cut off from his people; he hath broken my covenant.*
> (GENESIS: 17-14)

This is why Satan comes to you with all kinds of devices to trick you into breaking the covenant with your spouse, or with God. Your soul will be in bondage, torn away from

## COVENANT

your world. Do you see it? The implication of breaking a covenant? I advise you to always keep your part of a covenant. Never enter into a covenant of any kind when you are not sure. Whether good or bad, darkness or light, just take your time and think about what the word *covenant* really means. It is so powerful; it's even greater than the mere worldly terms of an agreement, promise, oath or contract between two parties.

Have you taken time to ask yourself why this is so important? Whenever you are newly employed at a firm, the company will first want you to sign a contract with them, prior to your starting work. While everyone knows the importance of a covenant, many are not aware of the spiritual power behind it.

Even today, some people get married and yet, after only a few months of marriage, they break the covenant they made to each other. After this, things start going wrong in their lives. They blame things they think might be the cause of their problem. They jump from one man or woman to another seeking happiness. Still, you can have peace, sister, brother. Stop going around in circles in your life. Your problem is not what you think it is. It may very well stem from a covenant that you broke a long time ago. Take stock of your life. If there's any false covenant speaking against you or undermining your family life, identify it, be prayerful and break it. Apply the three principles, shown through God's revelation to me, and set yourself free from this curse.

When someone signs an agreement or contract with a firm, they are legally bound by the rules and regulations of that company as set out in the agreement. If they break the rules that they agreed to abide by, the company has the (earthly) right to deal with the offender in a court of law. It is the same in the realm of the spirit. When someone enters into a covenant with Satan, he places that person into bondage. There are many ways to enter into a covenant with the devil without even knowing it. The first is through sin. It's an open door for the devil to come into your life. Once he succeeds, he gradually takes total control of your life. There are five means by which the devil enters into someone's life when they break a covenant. First, he manipulates them into breaking a covenant with their spouse or with God. Second, by breaking a covenant, you have sown a seed of sin in your life. What did God say about sin? It opens the door for the devil to come into your life. Third, the door remains open for devil to come into your life if you still don't do anything about it. The fourth step applies when the devil gradually takes control of your life. Once he succeeds in controlling your life, he takes the fifth step – he directs you down a wrong life path and, finally, to death.

*For when we were in the flesh, the motions of sins, which were by the law, did work in our members to bring forth fruit unto death.* (ROMAN: 7-5)

For example, if someone wants to initiate you into a secret society, they will first force you into entering into a covenant with them. It is the same in the kingdom of God. When you confess our Lord Jesus Christ as your personal saviour, you separate yourself from the earthly world into the kingdom of God. Now you are a new being. Old things pass away and new things come begging in your life.

*Therefore, if anyone is in Christ, he is a new creation. The old has passed away; behold, the new has come.* (2 CORINTHIANS 5:17)

But what if I have entered into a covenant and then I break it? How do I correct it so that this covenant won't speak against me?

*It is of the lord mercies that we are not consumed, because his compassions fail not.* (LAMENTATIONS 3:22)

Good question.

## First step

You need to call upon God Almighty and pray fervently for mercy. Confess all your sins at the altar of our merciful

God and pray with your whole heart to everlasting God to renew your spirit, and for His glory to come into your life.

## Second step

Seek out your covenanted partner. If you have found him or her, get on your knees and plead for mercy. Do all that is humanly possible to convince him or her to forgive you. Wait for them to say that they forgive you. Once he or she has told you this, heaven will record those words of forgiveness because the words we speak carry power.

## Third step

Offer him or her a gift as gratitude of thanksgiving.

Brethren, once you apply these three principles, I assure you will be cleansed and freed from the curse of the false covenant that speaks against you. Give God thanks and praise. Yes, it is simple, but powerful.

### PRAYER

**Dear Lord, you are God! Your covenant is trustworthy, and you have promised these good things to your servant. Now be pleased to bless the house of your servant, that it may continue forever in your sight; for you, Lord, have spoken, and with your blessing the house of your servant will be blessed forever.**

I pray for you right now that you will honor God by keeping your vow "until death separates".

SCRIPTURAL READINGS: 2 SAMUEL 7:28, ISAIAH 25:1, JOHN 3:17

. . .

# False Covenant

# False Covenant

• ✝ •

**The definition of a false covenant** can be an agreement entered into by deception in order to benefit from the covenanted party or person at their expense or disadvantage. It can also be defined as making a deal under a false pretence to gain something from man or God. This involves deceit, lies and falseness.

> *And I will give the men that have transgressed my covenant, which have not performed the words of the covenant which they had made before me, when they cut the calf in twain, and passed between the parts thereof, The princes of Judah, and the princes of Jerusalem, the eunuchs, and the priests, and all the people of the land, which passed between the parts of the calf; I will even give them into the hand of their enemies, and into the hand of them that seek their life: and their dead bodies shall be for meat unto the fowls of the heaven, and to the beasts of the earth.* (JEREMIAH: 34-18-19)

## THE COVENANT

Let's look at places in the Bible where false covenants have taken place, such as when the Gibeonites lived in Israel during the reign of King Saul. The Gibeonites entered into a covenant with Israel where they would be protected. But the covenant was broken and became a false one when King Saul, in his selfishness, decided to wipe the Gibeonites out of Israel.

Let us read about their story in 2 Samuel:

> *Then there was a famine in the days of David three years, year after year; and David enquired of the Lord. And the Lord answered, It is for Saul, and for his bloody house, because he slew the Gibeonites. And the king called the Gibeonites, and said unto them; (now the Gibeonites were not of the children of Israel, but of the remnant of the Amorites; and the children of Israel had sworn unto them: and Saul sought to slay them in his zeal to the children of Israel and Judah.)*
>
> *Wherefore David said unto the Gibeonites, What shall I do for you? And wherewith shall I make the atonement that ye may bless the inheritance of the Lord?*
>
> *And the Gibeonites said unto him, we will have no silver nor gold of Saul, nor of his house; neither for us shalt thou kill any man in Israel. And he said, what ye shall say, that will I do for you.*

*And there answered the king, The man that consumed us, and that devised against us that we should be destroyed from remaining in any of the coasts of Israel,*

*Let seven men of his sons be delivered unto us, and we will hang them up unto the Lord in Gibeah of Saul, whom the Lord did choose. And the king said, I will give them.*

*But the king spared Mephibosheth, the son of Jonathan the son of Saul, because of the Lord's oath mean (covenant) that was between them, between David and Jonathan the son of Saul.*
(2 SAMUEL: 21- 1-8)

Okay, let us pause here for a minute and begin to look at how powerful covenants are and the rewards that are due to those who diligently keep covenant. In scripture, Jonathan and David are examples of covenant-keepers. Saul is an example of a covenant-breaker, and his choice creates a false covenant. As we advance through this book's lessons, you will find some hidden truths about covenants and false covenants.

David and Jonathan made a covenant to each other to always be loyal, truthful, and helpful; to be each brother's keeper, even unto death. While still alive, Jonathan redeemed his own part of a covenant in order to help David during one of the most challenging periods in David's life.

Now we can see how powerful covenants are able to speak. Even after Jonathon's death, his covenant still spoke well of him. It extended blessings and protection to his son, Mephibosheth. According to the Bible, David spared Jonathon's son and blessed him because of the covenant he had entered into with his father Jonathan. Because of the sins committed by their forefathers, he gave up the rest of Saul's family to their enemy who slaughtered them.

There are some groups of people in this world for whom this false covenant still speaks against them in their lives. So many things have happened in their lives that they can't find any answers to their problems. They don't even know how it all started in the first place. They remain lost and confused. Some have already given up without a fight. The false covenants have succeeded in aborting their glory. When I say glory, I mean their God-given destiny, such as that which happened in the house of Saul. This was an example of how King Saul's family was cut off from the rest of the world.

There are some groups of people who have entered into a false covenant with a strange, demonic God in exchange for power. Some commit abominable sins in a quest to make money through evil means or selfish ways. They are unaware that by committing such a sin they have automatically entered into a false covenant with the devil in the realm of the spirit. They have given him a visa to dominate and control their life through evil ways. Torment becomes manifest in all areas of their life in exchange for power and wealth.

Don't get me wrong; power and wealth can be good – but the issue here is how you create wealth and power. Do you get wealth and power through good means, as our Lord Jesus Christ has taught us? Or through evil means?

The only way you can come out of any false covenant is to follow the footsteps of King David and to deal with the false covenant by praying to the Lord and asking for His help and guidance. Let us continue the story from 2 Samuel:

> *But the king took the two sons of Rizpah the daughter of Aiah, whom she bare unto Saul, Armoni and the five sons of Michal the daughter of Saul, whom she brought up for Adriel the son of Barzillai the Meholathite: And he delivered them into the hands of the Gibeonites, and they hanged them in the hill before the Lord: and they fell all seven together, and were put to death in the days of harvest, in the first days, in the beginning of barley harvest* (2 SAMUEL: 21-8-9)
>
> *Thus saith the Lord; If ye can break my covenant of the day, and my covenant of the night, and that*

*there should not be day and night in their season*
(JEREMIAH: 33-20)

Another example of a false covenant was between twin brothers Esau and Jacob *(see Genesis: 25-30-34)*.

According to the Bible's record of Jacob and Esau, Jacob had cooked some stew, and when Esau came in from the open fields, tired and hungry, he asked Jacob for some stew. But Jacob demanded Esau's birthright before he would share his food. Esau, who was exhausted to the point that he felt as if he was dying, could not see the need for his birthright at that time. He needed food. He pleaded with Jacob but Jacob demanded that Esau swear an oath to him. Desperate, Esau swore an oath to Jacob and sold him his birthright.

Heaven kept a record of the oath that Esau swore that day. Esau was unaware of the implications of that false covenant. He'd thought it was a joke. But his younger brother was clever and he meant business. He had deceived Esau into selling his birthright for a simple stew. My God, do you see it? He lost everything that day. I don't know how many of you have already sold your birthright into sin for just a moment's pleasure. There is a "get rich today and die tomorrow" way of doing business: selling drugs in the street; seeing prostitution as an easy way of making money; defrauding people around you. But these will not bring you any profit because you need to wait for the right time for your own blessing to come from God. Only these blessings will give you peace and joy in your life.

We are always in a rush to make money at any cost, without looking into whether the money we are making is giving life or destroying life, even during the process of making it. If you find yourself working in degenerate or deceptive ways of life, I advise you to turn away from such evil. The devil is at work in your life and he wants to steal everything God has given you. Note that a false covenant operates in your life once you open yourself to sin. Making money at any cost means you are automatically in covenant with the devil. You may not know it, but it's true. Sin is darkness and darkness is Satan. This is why I call it a *false covenant*.

Perhaps someone doesn't realise that the choices they have made in their life are an instrument of mass destruction used by Satan. For example, they may be a thief, a rapist, a drug dealer, a fraudster, a prostitute, or a false pastor posing as a real man of God, but deep inside, their heart is full of darkness. A false pastor may look like God on stage and they will preach the word of God, but they don't practise what they preach or teach. All their focus is on expanding their church and their pocket. If you fall into this category, you have already said 'yes' to the father of all lies, just as the Bible has called Satan the father of lies and sin. Brethren, change from your evil ways and come to the light. Ask the Lord God Almighty to break the false covenant that speaks against you and you will be freed from it.

The Bible tells us that Jacob gave Esau some bread and some lentil stew. Esau ate and drank, then got up and went out. So Esau despised his birthright. When we read Genesis 27, the Bible shows us the implications of Esau's mistake. Jacob also deceives their father Isaac into giving his father's blessing to him rather than to his older brother Esau. As a result of Esau selling his birthright to Jacob, Jacob stole Esau's blessing.

*His father Isaac asked, "Who are you?" "I am your firstborn son," he replied, "Esau!"*

*Isaac began to shake violently and asked, "Then who else hunted game and brought it to me? I ate all of it just before you arrived, and I blessed him. He will indeed be blessed!"*

*When Esau heard his father's words, he wailed loudly and bitterly. He said to his father, "Bless me too, my father!"*

*But Isaac replied, "Your brother came in here deceitfully and took away your blessing."*

*Esau exclaimed, "'Jacob' is the right name for him! He has tripped me up two times! He took away my birthright, and now, look, he has taken away my blessing!" Then he asked, "Have you not kept back a blessing for me?"*

*Isaac replied to Esau, "Look! I have made him lord over you. I have made all his relatives his servants and provided him with grain and new wine. What is left that I can do for you, my son?"*

*Esau said to his father, "Do you have only that one blessing, my father? Bless me too!" Then Esau wept loudly.*

*So his father Isaac said to him, "Indeed, your home will be away from the richness of the earth, and away from the dew of the sky above. You will live by your sword but you will serve your brother. When you grow restless, you will tear off his yoke from your neck."* (GENESIS 27)

But Jacob gets a taste of his own medicine. In Genesis 29, his uncle, Laban, makes a covenant with Jacob and promises that he can marry his daughter Rachel. But Laban then deceitfully sends his older daughter Leah to be Jacob's wife. By doing this, Laban makes a false covenant.

Brethren, understand that what goes around comes around. Entering into a false covenant with any person isn't right. If someone doesn't keep their promise, it will surely come back to haunt them. If you are not in love with him or her, why would you enter into a marriage covenant with him or her, knowing deep inside your heart that you don't really love him or her? You just want to use that person – perhaps because they have a good job and your financial needs will be met. When you are done with him or her you dump them like a waste product. Believe me, it will speak against you.

Don't joke around with your life. Covenants are very powerful. Don't allow the covenant you enter into to speak against you. When you break the covenant, it becomes false. The Bible warns us about what will happen if we break a covenant. I'm sure you wouldn't like to be cut off from this world; going around and around in circles, repeating events occurring in your life; all these things are signs of false covenants speaking against you.

A third example of where a false covenant has taken place in the Bible was Man's fall from grace in the Garden of Eden: the story of Adam and Eve.

> *And the Lord God commanded the man, saying, Of every tree of the garden thou mayest freely eat: But of the tree of the knowledge of good and evil, thou*

*shalt not eat of it: for in the day that thou eatest thereof thou shalt surely die.* (GENESIS: 2-16-17)

Breaking a covenant has serious consequences, causing damage and misery in our lives. It will continue to speak against us, generation after generation, until we do something about those false covenants at the altar of mercy and grace.

*Even when we were dead in sins, hath quickened us together with Christ, (by grace ye are saved).* (EPHESIANS: 2-5)

The first Adam messed up, but the second Adam came and redeemed us from sin and death through the blood shared on our behalf on the cross of Calvary. Through the cross, we have a second chance to repent from our sins when we acknowledge God as our Lord and personal saviour. He has told us that as many as will call on His name, He will give the power to become a son of God. Wow! Do you know what that means? It means we are God's ambassadors in the land of the living. Hallelujah.

## PRAYER

**Our Heavenly Father, show your mercy to me and gladden my heart. Forgive me for any covenant I have broken with You, or with any man or woman, knowingly or unknowingly, that speaks against**

**my life. I am like the sheep that went astray.**

**O Good Shepherd, seek me out and break every curse that speaks against my life, according to Your will. Let me dwell in Your house all the days of my life and praise You forever and ever. Amen.**

*Have mercy on me, O God, according to your unfailing love; according to your great compassion blot out my transgressions.* (PSALM: 51-1)

SCRIPTURAL READINGS: HEBREWS 4:16, LAMENTATIONS 3:22-23

• • •

# Covenant Relationships

# Covenant Relationships

• ✝ •

**In order for us to reach the next level** in our lives, we need to build a covenant relationship with God. As a believer, it is very important that we are in communion with God and that we continue to offer prayer each and every day of our lives. This builds the relationship with our Heavenly Father and then the light of God in our life will not run down. You see, the more you are in communion with Christ, the more you recharge the light of God in your life. This sets you up for a brighter future ahead. God is light, and anyone who believes in Christ has the light of God shine in them. This light needs to be recharged daily by reading the word of God (the Bible). I call it our life's menu.

God's plan for your life will be unveiled to you in time. It makes you walk along the correct path of the life ordained for you and your future. You see, the Bible is written from the inspiration of God's words and those words written are God. When you read the word of God, you are drawing strength from His words into your spirit – hallelujah – and that strength is God. It will abide in you. The Bible tells us that if you abide in God, he will equally abide in you. We are joint heirs of Christ Jesus. Clothed with the heavenly body, we are imperishable seeds of God set to rise. By the gospel of our Lord Jesus Christ in the land of the living. Hallelujah.

> *If you abide in me, and my words abide in you, ask whatever you wish, and it shall be done for you.*
> (JOHN: 15-7)

The word of God comes alive in you when the covenant relationship with Him is operating in your life. God is in your thoughts, your character, your direction; your step is in line with God's word. This brings you success in all of your life's endeavours.

Let us briefly look at Isaac's life as told to us in the Bible. A covenanted relationship operated through Isaac's life-journey with God. Isaac maintained his covenant relationship with God and this resulted in tremendous blessings in his life.

The Bible records in Genesis 26:1-32:

> *There was a famine in the land, besides the first famine that was in the days of Abraham his father. And Isaac went unto Abimelech king of the Philistines unto Gerar.*
>
> *Then the Lord appeared to Isaac and said Do not go down to Egypt live in the land I promised your father and your descendants. Dwell in this land, and I will be with you and bless you, for to you and*

*your descendants I give all these lands, and I will perform the covenant which I swore to Abraham your father. And I will make your descendants multiply as the stars of heaven I will give to your descendants all these lands and in your seed all the nations of the earth shall be blessed, because Abraham your father obeyed My voice and My covenant, My statutes, and My laws.*

*Then Isaac obeyed God and sowed in that land, and reaped in the same year a hundredfold and the Lord blessed him. And he began to prosper, and continued prospering until he became very prosperous for he had possessions of flocks and possessions of herds and a great number of servants. So the Philistines envied him. The Philistines had stopped up all the wells which his father's servants had dug in the days of Abraham his father, and they had filled them with earth. And Abimelech said to Isaac, "Go away from us, for you are much mightier than we."*

*Then Isaac departed from there and pitched his tent in the Valley of Gerar, and dwelt there. Isaac dug again the wells of water which they had dug in the days of Abraham his father, for the Philistines had stopped them up after the death of Abraham. He called them by the names which his father had called them.*

Isaac became a very wealthy, influential and prominent man in the land. Even his enemy, Abimelech, who was afraid, could see that Isaac was blessed by the Lord so he made peace with Isaac.

You see, brethren, it pays to be in a covenant relationship with our Lord Jesus Christ. Let's look into this covenant relationship in another way – with humans, in the world we live in. Understanding the importance of covenant relationships in our life is the will of God for our life. There are people God has joined together who are there to impart into and impact on our lives so we can do what God has called us to do. It may be their wisdom, their expertise or their knowledge that can help us, or it may be a specific anointing in their lives that God wants to develop in us.

Ecclesiastes 4:9-12 says something very interesting...

*Two are better than one. Because they have a good reward for their labour. For if they fall, the one will lift up his fellow: but woe to him that is alone when he falleth; for he hath not another to help him up. Again, if two lie together, then they have heat: but how can one be warm alone? And if one prevail against him, two shall withstand him; and a threefold cord is not quickly broken.*

The Bible even talks about how God is in the midst of

believers when they come together. Relationships are the lifeblood of human existence. So I encourage you, brethren, to keep and always maintain a covenant relationship with man and with God throughout your life.

SCRIPTURAL READING: JUDGES 2:1-3; GENESIS 15; GALATIANS 3:13-14; ROMANS 3:26; ROMANS 8:1.

COVENANT SCRIPTURE: GENESIS: 15; JEREMIAH: 34-18-19, JOSHUA: 9-6-15; 1 SAMUEL 20-8, PROVERB: 2:17; MATTHEW 18:11-35

We trust God to empower us to keep this unity of love, no matter the cost.

• • •

# Prayer

# Prayer

• ☦ •

**Brethren, before we start praying**, I will share with you briefly the importance of prayer in your life. When you pray, you are not only praying to our Lord Jesus Christ, but you are also in fellowship and have communion with the Holy Spirit. You tap into the realm of the spirit where God can speak directly to you.

> *Praying always with all prayer and supplication in the spirit, and watching thereunto with all perseverance and supplication for all saint: And for me, that utterance may be given unto me that I may speak boldly, as I ought to speak.* (EPHESIANS: 6-18-19)

You see, brethren, God wants us as believers to pray daily always in spirit. The Bible tells us that when we pray in tongues, we are communicating with God in spirit, and your spirit is in one with Christ. Throughout my research in the Bible, it is clear that the greatest men and women God has used are people who knew how to pray, and those great people understood how prayer is necessary in all their life's endeavours.

> *Truly, truly, I say to you, he who believes in me, the works that I do shall he do also and greater works than these shall he do because I go to the father. And whatever you ask in my name, that will I do, that the father may be glorified in the son.* (JOHN 14:12-13)

Prayer requires faith in all things. Whatever you ask for in prayer, you need to believe you will receive it.

> *Jesus answered and said unto them, verily I say unto you, if ye have faith, and doubt not, ye shall not only do this which is done to the fig tree, but also if ye shall say unto this mountain, be thou removed, and be thou cast into the sea, it shall be done. And all things, whatsoever ye shall ask in prayer, believing, ye shall receive.* (MATTHEW: 21-21-22)

Please pray with me…

**Dear Heavenly Father, I pray for your mercy.**
**Have mercy on me.**
**Listen to my prayer for mercy as I cry out to you for help,**
**As I lift my hands toward your holy sanctuary.**
**Look kindly upon me and have mercy on me so**

that in time of difficult moments we might not
despair nor become despondent,
but with great confidence submit ourselves to
your holy will,
which is love and mercy.
Lord Jesus, I come before you just as I am.
Lord Jesus, I kneel before you.
I am sorry for all my sins.
I am sorry for my disobedience.
I am sorry for my evil ways.
I repent all of my sins. Please forgive me.
In the name of Jesus, as I forgive all others for
what they have done against me.
I renounce Satan, the evil spirits and all their
works.
I give you my entire self, Lord Jesus, now and
forever.
I invite you into my life, Jesus.
I accept you as my Lord, God and Saviour.
Heal every part of my body.
Deliver me.
Deliver me from all satanic traps.
Clean me.
Break every spiritual chain used by Satan and his
cohorts in all areas of my life.
Wash me with the blood of Jesus.
Strengthen me, my body, my soul, my spirit.

## THE COVENANT

**Come, Lord Jesus, and cover me with your precious blood.**
**Protect me from all evil attacks.**
**Fill me with your holy spirit.**
**I love, I love, I love you, Lord Jesus.**
**I praise your holy name, Jesus.**
**Sweet Jesus, I praise you.**
**I thank you, Jesus.**
**I shall follow you every day of my life. Amen.**

. . .

# Vision

• ✝ •

**My vision is to raise an army of true believers** to help rid the world of evil. If you have faith and you believe in Christ, you can be freed from the bondage of satanic influences and transgressions by following Christ's message, using the power of prayer and the word of God (the Bible) to open the prison gate of any mind bound by Satan. By prayer and by understanding the revelations from God's words, you will be set free from all kinds of bondage and influence in your life by Satan. The forces of Satan are everywhere, trying to corrupt and deceive people, but by choosing the right path of worshipping God and rejecting Satan and his wiles, we will overcome them.

• • •

## If you feel that God is calling you

to be a supporter or a participant of this vision, write to me at:
**davidajaere@risingofGodarmy.co.uk**

Say, "David Ajaere, I am in support of God's vision in your life."

www.ingramcontent.com/pod-product-compliance
Lightning Source LLC
Chambersburg PA
CBHW032052290426
44110CB00012B/1055